WAKE UP YOUR SLEEPING GIANT

A Working Professional's Guide to Optimizing Morning Time for Success.

Enhance Productivity at Work and Climb Up the Corporate Ladder.

GYAN S NARAYAN

Thank You: Your Free Gift

As a token of my thanks for taking out time to read my book, I would like to offer you a free gift:

Acquaint yourself with a time breakup of 60 minutes of morning rituals that will:

1. Completely Transform yourself
2. Bring good health
3. Make you wealthy
4. Make you happy
5. Bring concentration power
6. Bring calmness within you
7. Develop book reading habit
8. Plan your day

Email me at gyansnarayan22@gmail.com **and mention Free Gift in the subject.**

Table of Contents

Chapter One

Introduction

> **"Words may inspire but only action creates change."**
>
> **-Simon Sinek**

Because of the immense pressure today's hectic lifestyle puts on us, we are all caught up in life's whirlpool of events, where we let life lead us where it may.

In this scenario, you as a professional with a sales job, marketing job, administrative job, or even as an MNC executive or Corporate CEO, you find yourself doing what you deem to be necessary. Yet, you cannot find much-needed time for yourself. Even when you can identify something that would be of benefit to you, somehow life comes in between and you have to abandon the idea. Incidentally, you are not the only one in this universe facing such a challenge of life-work balance.

Many professionals are unable to develop their careers while still keeping their social life vibrant. A good number of professionals have no social life at all. This is the main problem many professionals face, and successive generations are passing through this challenge. You are facing this problem, but you feel helpless.

You feel like there is nothing you can do to change your lifestyle, yet you want to dedicate ample time to your family, don't you? This book is for you. The book will try to solve this very serious problem for you. Without a doubt, you will be a changed person after reading this book.

Discover the Hidden Giant in You!

You will discover in this book a giant hidden within you, just waiting for you to activate it to do wonders for you. You have infinite potential that you are not aware of, and it will be revealed to you in later chapters.

Everyone in this universe has problems, whether he is a company CEO, a multi-billionaire, or a working professional, but the difference is that a successful person knows how to cope with the problems.

How to emerge victorious

Does overcoming a problem require a change of mindset? Do you have a fixed mindset or a growth mindset? You may not know the answers to these questions, but you will learn them as you read through the chapters of this book. You will get to know the truth behind the different mindsets, and how you can cultivate a growth mindset which can give a different lens to the problem you are going through.

Are you a professional aspiring for promotion in your job? Are you a professional who wants to have more energy to guide your team? Are you a professional unable to meet your sales target and wants to do so? Are you a professional who wants to climb up the corporate ladder much faster than your colleagues?

As a top management professional in your organization, do you lack the energy to influence your joint venture partners? The problems are many, but in essence they are really not insurmountable problems. You just need some tightening of the nuts and bolts of your brain.

Really, what I have just said is true! These are all not real problems, but the result of a fixed mindset that you still have not managed to change. Nevertheless, there is nothing to worry about as now you are in good hands. This book you have in your hand will mentor you and help you change yourself, and at the end of the day bring you the success you deserve.

Many a time, we feel like we do not have sufficient time to do what we want. But is this so? If you think it is, ask yourself why there are so many successful people in every field.

Have you ever thought why there are successful millionaires and Billionaires? They do not have more than 24 hours in a day. They have challenges just like you, but they are more successful today than you are. Why? There must be some secret measures they are taking that you are unaware of. Would you like to know those secrets?

I will walk you through the secrets of a successful person. The first one is the mantra: "If anyone can do it successfully, you, too, can do it".

Success always leaves clues, and you need to follow those clues for you to succeed. As I will reveal in subsequent chapters, you have infinite potential and you only need a spark to ignite that sleeping giant within yourself. I will reveal to you the characteristics of successful people, and if you copy them, you will join the list of successful personalities the world keeps discussing.

Research shows that faith, burning desire, and consistency, abbreviated as FBC, will move the mountains. Roger Bannister, a renowned athlete, had a clear vision of becoming the best runner in the world. He wanted to set a record of running one mile in under four minutes, and he had faith in his vision. Such a feat was not humanly possible, and many doctors in his town told him as much. However,

Bannister maintained his focus, by sheer determination he was able to make the record.

Roger Bannister had dreamt of his victory and ensured he practised intensely. Every day, he woke up at 4 am and practised. In his mind, he had no doubt he would win the milestone. The entire universe witnessed the impressive run on May 6th 1954, when Roger Bannister broke the world record as per his vision to the surprise of all the doctors., he had achieved, managed to set a record of running 1 mile in 3 minutes and 54 seconds!

How was this possible? Was it a miracle? Obviously, it was an extraordinary feat, but Roger Bannister's first stepping stone to success was his determination to succeed. He believed in his capacity to win the race and break the world record, and he developed a burning desire to fulfill his vision.

He was consistent in his daily practice and this determination and discipline brought him laurels. He received many accolades and the entire universe congratulated him. Some people even told him he was lucky, yet Bannister knew the harsh reality. His success was not a single-day effort but a consistent and persistent effort. It was his dedication and consistency in waking up at 4 am every morning to start practice that made him succeed.

Think about a similar situation in your life. You can also be like Roger Bannister in your field. You can achieve whatever you wish in your career as long as you have the determination. Today, as a working professional, you might find it difficult to meet your targets, and you feel uncomfortable to attend business review presentations.

When you are questioned about the business deficit you can only answer "Definitely, in the coming quarter"; or "next month I'll achieve the target". Yet month after month you keep finding yourself in the same situation. At the same time, some of your colleagues are able to achieve their targets, and they receive great feedback from the top management during review meetings. What makes the difference between you and those who meet their targets?

For example, if you are a sales professional, you may think your counterparts succeed because their territories have more potential or their products are in higher demand. Similarly, a few Heads of the Corporate Verticals might attract reviews during business meetings while others get laurels for their work. Why does this happen?

Why is there always a blue-eyed boy of the top management? There must be some game-changing rules that some people follow and others do not. But do not worry. This book contains deep research regarding the activities of a successful person, which the author has carefully verified.

Yes, I have put into practice the success methods discussed in this book as an experiment on myself, and I have found a sea change in my personality. My well-being has also greatly improved. As I continue my journey of success, I assure you that if you follow and practice the principles taught in this book, you will be a changed personality with numerous successes. In short, **you will realize the hidden potential within you that was asleep till now.**

I call this hidden potential your **"SLEEPING GIANT"**.

This book is a masterpiece with plenty of research work. It is the second in a series already started, with the first book being, "Grab your Victory Hour". That first book, by this same author, has been hailed by readers for having brought a positive change in their lives.

The first chapter of this book, "Wake up your Sleeping Giant", talks about the "the power of the morning hour". In this chapter, you will realize how beautiful morning hours are and how much you have been missing all these days by not taking advantage of those golden hours; the early hours of the day that set the tone for your day.

The second chapter talks about "Setting the stage for success and preparing you for the morning routine". You will learn how to utilize the morning hour and make yourself ready for the aggressive fight of the day. This is the kind of fight that makes you motivated to the extent of appearing aggressive in your work. With such intense motivation, you will progress much faster in your professional career.

The third Chapter is about "Mindset Matters: How to start your day with a positive attitude", and it gives insights into eight morning rituals that will completely transform you. These rituals guarantee you mental and physical energy, which then help you to take complete charge of your day. The kind of mental energy you generate is necessary when your aim is to climb the corporate ladder.

The fourth chapter is on "Productivity Hacks: Maximizing your time and efficiency". This chapter reveals the secret to optimizing your time and increasing efficiency in your work. You will learn how to concentrate on your work efficiently, and this level of efficiency will give you immense satisfaction.

The fifth chapter talks about "Planning and Prioritization: Organizing your tasks and goals", and how essential these two Ps are to achieving victory in your life. They are also essential to achieving any target, be it in sales, marketing, administration, business ventures, and the like. In this chapter, you will learn how to apply important principles in your work, making a great difference in your functioning.

This book promises to awaken the sleeping giant within you, and to bring you loads of success and good fortunes by changing your personality. The book targets working professionals who want to streamline their office work, make progress in their career, and quickly climb up the corporate ladder.

I wish you good luck!

Key takeaways

- "If anyone can do it successfully, you, too, can do it".
- Success always leaves clues, and you need to follow those clues for you to succeed.
- Faith, burning desire, and consistency, abbreviated as FBC, will move the mountains.
- You have a hidden potential within you that was asleep till now. This hidden potential is your **"SLEEPING GIANT"**. You can awaken it.

Chapter Two

The Power of the Morning Hour

> **"Morning is an important time of the day because how you spend your morning can often tell you what kind of day you are going to have.**
>
> **-Lemony Snicket**

"The early bird catches the worm" is a well-known saying that has a lot of truth in real life. Morning time is the best for revitalizing yourself to get the most output. Who does not want sufficient energy to carry him/her through a busy day?

Suppose you are a professional salesperson, marketer, HR, or operations officer; you need energy to perform your office work and guide your team to achieve the target the organization has set. But the question is how to get that treasure where you have enough energy to perform your tasks. Eating and sleeping may not provide the requisite energy and put you in the right mindset to achieve your goals.

Of course, eating and sleeping energizes you, but they do not help you generate sufficient power to attend to your work – at least not enough to give you the extra punch required to achieve excellence in your career. Unless you do something else besides eating and sleeping, you will always feel deficient and not able to go the extra mile needed to achieve excel in your work. Why is this the case?

Research shows that our body and mind do not operate well without a routine. Anything haphazard in life often confuses your mind and brain, and your body only does what is essential to keep you going.

One fact is that all successful people habitually wake up early in the morning. Bill Gates, for example, wakes up at 5 am, while Richard Branson and Apple CEO Tim Cook, the CEO of Apple wake up at 5.30 am and 3.45 am respectively.

You can find many more great personalities who have the habit of waking up early, but do you know the secret behind this early rising? In this chapter, I will reveal to you how your mind and body dynamics can change simply by getting into the habit of waking up early.

Successful people align their minds and bodies with nature. They break down the day's 24 hours into four parts –early morning, official working hours, evening family time, and sleep time. This routine is in alignment with the flow of Mother Nature, as Nature's 24-hour schedule is divided into four parts.

Research shows that if you align your body with mother nature, your mind and body will be in sync, and your life will be balanced. In my book "Grab Your Victory Hour", I have dedicated my research to the morning rituals one should adopt after waking up, in order to have a fulfilling day. The book gives excellent insights of the 60-minute rituals one should perform every morning in order to become an extraordinarily great performer.

Waking up early in the morning as a matter of habit is not an uphill task. You just need to be determined and to have the right mindset. If you are not in the habit of waking up early in the morning, then you are missing out on the most beautiful part of your day – the serenity of the morning hours, the chirping sound of birds, the cool breeze of fresh air and a lot more. Once you develop the habit of waking up in the morning, you will be addicted to it and will find it difficult to skip an early morning. I can bet you on this. If you miss to wake up early any day, you will feel something missing. That is the beauty of the early morning habit. In due course, you will appreciate the power that comes with rising up early, and the positive energy around the experience.

Waking up early gives you more time to plan your day and get things done. Research has shown that people who wake up early are more productive than those who wake up later in the day. Early risers enjoy the following health benefits:

1. Better mental health: Studies show that waking up early is associated with better mental health, including lower stress levels, anxiety, and depression.
2. Improved sleep quality: Going to bed early and waking up just as early regularly each

day can help regulate your body's internal clock and improve the quality of your sleep.

3. Better physical health: People who wake up early tend to be more active and ready to engage more in physical activity. This habit often has a range of health benefits, including reduced risk of obesity, diabetes, and heart disease.

4. More time for self-care: Waking up early accords you sufficient time to take care of yourself, whether you want to exercise, meditate, or enjoy a quiet cup of coffee before the day starts.

Overall, research suggests that waking up early can positively impact your physical and mental health, as well as your productivity and overall quality of life.

I have personally experienced the immense benefits that come with waking up early in the morning. The energy you gain end up taking you on a different trajectory altogether. I have read many books about successful people, and also listened to many podcasts on the subject. I can say with confidence that morning is the best time to give you clarity of thought, and so I would urge you stake a claim on your morning and enjoy much needed "ME" time.

This golden time helps you to know yourself, understand what you want in life, and spend time with yourself with rituals like exercise, meditation, reading motivational books and many more. In my next chapter, I will elaborate on all these aspects of morning rituals, giving you detailed perspectives of 8 morning rituals with a specific time of devotion for every ritual. If you perform these rituals consistently, you will witness a sea change in your outlook towards life.

There is a lot of truth in the assertion that sacrifice is required to achieve anything significant in life. Nothing happens by chance. You must have a Burning desire to achieve your dreams. As a working professional, you will have a workflow to keep you busy the entire day. When you enter the office in the morning, you are immersed in a whirlpool of activities, and after 8-10 hours of hard work you realize evening has come. It is fine that you work hard and are involved in the day's processes, but has it ever occurred to you that you need to devote a few hours to your well-being as well?

You may argue that life is too hectic to allow you enjoy personal time. You consistently sleep late and find it difficult to rise up in the morning, and as a result you remain in a cycle of sleeping and waking up late. You wake up only early enough for you to rush to the office, and on reaching the office your journey for the day starts with meetings, reviews, discussions about targets and so on. This is the lifestyle of 90% of the working professionals, who have surrendered themselves to their fate. They are just moving toward where life takes them. They think they have no choice but to continue their daily office-home routine, and they term this life cycle as their fate. Getting a job promotion and a salary increment becomes their target, and as they pursue this carrot of life, they end up compromising their health.

Along the journey, these professionals may amass wealth, purchase houses of their dreams on a Loan and pay EMI that they pay for throughout their lives.

The big question is: What do you have beyond that mundane lifestyle?

One day you will realize you have spent 20-30 years of your life running around your job because you let life dictate what you do. Consider the stress and anxiety you are experiencing in your current lifestyle, where it is easy to gain weight, and have a rise in blood pressure and sugar. These are the by-products of your hard work. Hard work is always good, for certain, but it should not be at the cost of your health. I will guide you in this book on how to increase your work productivity and mind your well-being at the same time.

It is worthwhile mentioning that after you retire from your job your health will be your only friend. You will only enjoy your life if you are in good health. It is good health that will help you enjoy the assets and wealth you will have created during your lifetime. If your health fails you, all the years of hard work will be in vain and you will feel guilty about not having paid attention to your well-being when you were younger.

The time to bring a balance into your life is during your youthful years. It is rightly said that "Health is Wealth". In short, without health wealth is useless. That is why you need to understand the power and benefits of morning hours and to make utmost use of them.

Note that successful people not only wake up early in the morning, but they have a set routine for their daily activities. In my next chapter, I will walk you through the eight rituals you must do as a matter of routine, so as to make your morning brighter, and your entire day extra promising and productive.

I have personally practised the rituals involved. Each of these processes effectively unblocks your mind one after the other, and you can immediately feel the difference. I can assure you that once you adapt to the morning routine discussed in the next chapter, you will drastically improve your personality and be among the 1% of world's successful people. In other words, you will have mastered the art of success.

Key takeaways

Waking up early can positively impact your physical and mental health as well as your productivity and overall quality of life. Research has shown that waking up early in the morning can have a variety of benefits:

1. Increased productivity: Waking up early gives you more time to plan your day and get things done. Research has shown that people who wake up early are more productive than those who wake up later in the day.

2. Better mental health: Waking up early is associated with better mental health, including lower stress levels, anxiety, and depression.

3. Improved sleep quality: Going to bed and waking up at the same time every day can help regulate your body's internal clock and improve the quality of your sleep.

4. Better physical health: People who wake up early tend to be more active and they engage in more physical activity, which often comes with a range of health benefits

- reduced risk of obesity, diabetes, and heart disease.

5. More time for self-care: Waking up early accords you more time to take care of yourself, whether you want to exercise, meditate, or simply enjoy a quiet cup of coffee before you start your day.

6. Learn 8 morning rituals that will completely transform you.

Chapter Three

Setting the Stage for Success: Preparing for Your   Morning Routine

> **"The secret of making progress is to get started".**
>
> **Mark Twain**

Developing any habit requires determination to change yourself from within. This determination is purely your responsibility. You can achieve anything in your life if you decide to. Author Tony Robbins says you can instantly change your life if you take an instant DECISION. That DECISION you take will transform you and you will never wish to look backwards. Even if you are a night owl and find it difficult to wake up in the morning, or you have been sleeping late consistently for years, this is a habit you can change.

Everything you want to accomplish is linked to your mind. Nothing can shake your will to wake up early if you have set your mind to being up and about before dawn. Initially, you may find it uncomfortable, which is quite natural considering you are trying to get out of your comfort zone. However, soon you are going to adjust to your new life and appreciate the beautiful journey.

Many of you may be wondering why you should abandon the habit of sleeping late. You might question the logic. You would think: Sleeping late and getting up late has been your habit for the last 20 years and more, and rising late gives you a feeling of freshness.

It is quite normal to feel that way when your habit has been with you for a long 20 years, because you will have established a comfort zone. There is a shell around that zone within which you relax and stay contented. But you need to ask yourself: How are my body's metabolic functions faring? What is my rhythmic sleep cycle? What is the digestion pattern of my body? Questions of this nature will help you see the logic behind changing your life habits.

Medical science has proved that many biological processes happen during sleep. The brain stores new information and gets rid of toxic waste during this period. Nerve cells communicate and reorganize themselves, and these functions help to enhance your brain function.

It is at night while you sleep that the body repairs cells, restores energy, and releases molecules of hormones and proteins. Between 11 pm and 3 am, we have more NREM (non-rapid eye movement) sleep than any other time, and this is essential for the restoration and healing of our organs.

From 3 am to 7 am, we are more likely to get REM (rapid eye movement) sleep, characterized by vivid dreams. So, those who habitually sleep late miss out on the restorative sleep hour, which falls between 11 pm to 6 am.

Today, you may be enjoying your sleep pattern, but your body will soon require a change. Waking up early in the morning has many benefits, and you should aim at taking maximum advantage of them.

Seek to maximize the benefits of your victory hour the moment you wake up. And which is that hour?

Your victory hour is the first hour after your wake up in the morning. If you are in the habit of sleeping late, you should gradually change that habit. Initially, try going to bed 30 minutes earlier than usual, and compensate for those 30 minutes by waking up 30 minutes earlier than usual. You will soon realize you are getting some extra free time, and you can do whatever you want with that time. You can go for a walk, go swimming, exercise, meditate, read a book, or whatever else might interest you. In addition, your productivity during the day is bound to increase.

Nevertheless, you will initially face two challenges; one is that your body will resist retiring and rising early, and the other is that your mind will try to reject the new routine. But you have to break this mind-and-body resistance because, ultimately find peace with yourself in your newfound world.

Your new routine will enable you discover a new personality. You will begin to feel great change within you. With your changed habits , you will awaken your sleeping giant, and you can expect it to perform wonders for you.

Yes, in case you were not aware, you do have a giant lying within you but in a dormant state. This giant has enough potential to move you to newer heights, enabling you to be the most intelligent, systematic, and able performer. You have immense hidden power within you that you are yet to discover. In the words of Swami Vivekananda, "All power is within you; you can do anything and everything. Believe in that, do not believe that you are weak; do not believe that you are half-crazy lunatics, as most of us do nowadays. You can do anything and everything, without even the guidance of any one. Stand up and express the divinity within you."

Yes, we all have immense power within, but we fail to recognize the hidden strengths within us because it is dormant. You need to activate yours, and then you can find yourself a new personality. Certainly, the key to activating your sleeping giant is your "MIND" and the "DECISION" you make to change your habits.

I have read many books on morning habits and listened to many podcasts on how to change your sleeping and waking habits, and even on the benefits of waking up early morning and I can vouch that waking up early morning changes your mindset and your personality. You end up having a positive outlook on life, and you feel that the same world is now a better place to live.

Developing the good morning wake-up habits requires discipline, and a particular technique to ensure you remain consistent. Every success requires preparation, and so if you plan on waking up early in the morning, you need to prepare yourself the night before. This preparation starts with you adopting the right mindset, and a firm determination to forge forward with your new lifestyle and not look back. Even if you feel a strong urge to resist waking up when you want to, do not snooze the alarm. Do not fall victim to such a temptation that requires you to remain in your comfort zone. Do please keep your focus and remember you want to break your old sleep habit and replace it with a great new one. This new habit will be part of the lifestyle that will take you to greater heights if you accept to make the necessary sacrifice.

Author Tony Robbins has rightly said that our actions are distributed between "PAIN" and "PLEASURE". Any action we take in our lives is either because pleasure is involved or we avoid it because pain is involved. There is no third option. But if we convert the pain involved in the process into pleasure, we can easily change our mindset and take positive action. Waking up in the morning is a pain for you because for years you have been enjoying the use of your snooze button. You have continuously derived pleasure from its use, and it is tough for your mind and body to abandon the pleasure and go through the pain your body is being asked to endure – that of waking up early and leaving your cosy bed.

Still, if you associate that same pain with the pleasure correspondingly associated with morning rituals, which I will talk about in detail in the next chapter, the realization will alter your mindset. Hence, you will find it easy to abandon the old form of pleasure.

This is, certainly, very true. Try it today. This pain and pleasure mindset is true for any activity we engage in. Once you have decided to wake up early in the morning, the next important step is to fix the time. Most successful people wake up between 4.00 am and 6 am. Set your alarm for the time it suits you initially, either 5.30 a.m. or 6 a.m. and wake up every day at that same time. You must wake up at the first ring without giving room for the slightest temptation to press the alarm snooze button. To achieve your goal, keep the alarm clock a good distance from your bed. This way, you will have to rise up and walk if you want to stop the alarm.

Still, do not look back at your bed once you have risen. Instead, leave the bedroom, go to the kitchen, and immediately take a glass of water. You may also take lukewarm water if you prefer it. Drinking a glass of water at this time will immediately hydrate your body, as your body loses water content after a span of 6 - 7 hours of sleep. Research shows that during sleep our body loses its water content and so, taking a glass of water immediately after waking up hydrates and energizes you. In my book "Grab Your Victory Hour", I have recommended the following morning rituals be followed during the Victory Hour for 60 minutes:

1. Sweating Exercise for 15 minutes
2. Breathing Exercise for 5 minutes
3. Affirmation for 5 minutes
4. Visualization for 5 minutes
5. Meditation for 5 minutes
6. Reading books for 10 minutes
7. Journaling for 5 minutes
8. Planning for 10 minutes

After thorough research and various studies, I have made the above rituals to be followed in the order from 1 to 8. The above habits are potent weapons experimented with and followed by me for the last five years. The ritual routine is enriching, as long as you complete the above practices. I cannot emphasize enough how one feels by the end of these rituals. You need to experience it and let me know via my email id gyansnarayan22@gmail.com.

Key takeaways

- Set the alarm time that suits you initially, either for 5.30 a.m. or 6 a.m. and wake up every day at the same time.

- You, must wake at the ring of the first alarm without succumbing to the slightest temptation to press the snooze button.

- Keep the alarm clock a distance away from your bed so that it is inconvenient to walk up to the alarm and silence it.

- Ensure you do not look back at your bed after you have risen. Instead, leave the bedroom and straightway go to the kitchen and take a glass of water.

- Drinking a glass of water after you wake up will immediately hydrate and energize your body, which is crucial as your body loses water content after a span of 6 - 7 hours of sleep.

Chapter Four

Mindset Matters: How to start your day with a Positive Attitude

> **"Believe you can and you're halfway there".**
>
> **Theodore Roosevelt**

Starting your day with a positive attitude can set the tone for the rest of the day and help increase productivity and overall well-being. As working professionals, you need to start your day in the right frame of mind to be more productive. You might have noticed sometimes you have mood swings; some days you feel good and other days you feel gloomy. Nevertheless, your mindset needs to be more consistent.

Ask yourself why you are not.

As a working professional, you might be in a leadership position, in middle management, or even among the core workforce of your organization. Your position must justify the position you hold and bring in the best to the organization. But often, you are not able to accomplish this because you are not in the right frame of mind.

Sometimes you have grand plans for your work but feel like you are too shallow to achieve the task. Why does this happen? Why do you feel sluggish? Why are you not internally motivated to take complete charge of the day? Your team members or clients expect to see some radiance on your face – a face full of energy. When your body language portrays energy, everyone around you feels that energy too and benefits from it. They draw some energy from you and they become vibrant. Consequently, they think of you as a charismatic leader whose immense energy lasts the entire day.

When your colleagues enter the office and see a spark on your face, they feel motivated and energized. They are also impressed to see that you have the same energy level in the evening as you had in the morning. Don't you long to have that radiant face and have your body language set a positive direction for your colleagues? When you are vibrant with positive energy, your colleagues see a leader in you, and beyond that they enjoy your company. It is a great feeling achieving this stature in the office, where your superiors and co-workers respect you and see potential for leadership in you.

Yet you have to get into the habit of waking up early every day for all this to be possible. All successful entrepreneurs are morning people who have developed a habit of waking up at a fixed time every morning. They derive their energy from the morning rituals they religiously perform every day. You, too, can become a successful professional and rise to the top of your career if you discipline yourself with the morning rituals that I discuss in this chapter.

Let me highlight a few facts that will affirm the claims I make here. Note that the rituals I have compiled after dedicated research and practice ought to be followed in the order given below:

A. Sweating Exercise (15 Minutes)

The first-morning ritual in your victory hour is "Exercise". Research shows that our brain is initially slow and less receptive when we wake up. But then, if aggravated, it does wonders. I have read many books, listened to many podcasts, and attended several seminars on morning habits. Every podcast and book teach and recommend that you fix your morning routine to suit you. After conducting research and experiments, I found that you must begin your day by doing EXERCISE, and the best activity being dancing to music of your choice. You should aim to sweat it out as you tune in and dance to the music.

As you begin exercising, depending on the intensity, various essential chemical messengers called neurotransmitters are released throughout your nervous system, giving you a positive feeling. Researchers have found that aerobic exercise produces endorphins, or "feel good" chemicals, and also increases your heart rate. These events trigger the release of norepinephrine, a chemical that helps the brain deal with stress more effectively. Also, exercise

helps to increase blood flow into the brain.

I know from personal experience that once you dance and jump to music your heart rate increases and your mind becomes alert. You feel your brain opening and notice everything around you looking bright. On the overall, exercising produces a feel-good factor that you experience from within.

Allocate 15 minutes to exercising, and make use of a mobile timer to ensure that every activity is given the right amount of time. I guarantee you if you keep to this preset routine, you will enjoy your exercise session even as you dance to your favorite music. Sweat it out by enjoying doing what you like, which could be even walking, hiking, or running. Any movement-related physical exercise done over 15 minutes is very helpful. The idea is to have yourself sweat. This is the first principle for a good start.

B. Breathing Exercise: (5 minutes)

The second-morning ritual within your victory hour is the "Breathing Exercise". It is a known fact that no living being can exist without breathing. We exist because we can breathe. My question is- Do we appreciate the importance of breathing or are we conscious of our breathing when we take in and take out air? Unfortunately, we don't. Mostly we take this process for granted because it happens naturally. And so, we wonder: Why should we bother about what happens naturally? This is generally everyone's way of thinking.

Breathing is a subconscious function. When we are sleep, our breathing continues as usual and this process is not about to change. But if we devote some time to feeling our breath, we might realize the importance of breathing and further leverage its benefit to improve our life. For this reason, I suggest you engage in a "breathing exercise" every day for 5 minutes.

The breathing technique I recommend involves sitting down in a quiet place with your back straight, after which you start to consciously and calmly inhale and exhale air. You can sit on the floor with your legs crossed or on a chair, wherever you feel comfortable. You then need to place your right thumb on the right nostril and inhale air deeply from the left nostril.

Hold your breath for a few seconds, place your right middle finger on the left nostril, and then exhale the air from the right nostril.

Next, with your right middle finger placed on the left nostril, inhale deeply from the right nostril. Hold your breath for a few seconds and then by placing the right thumb on the right nostril, you can exhale from the left nostril. Breathing in and out once constitutes one cycle of the exercise, and you can repeat the cycle ten times. Eventually you will feel some soothing vibration in your brain, which has a calming effect.

I have been practising this breathing exercise for the last five years, and it gives me immense energy from within and much clarity of thought. You, too, can enjoy this feeling of purity if you take up this exercise as part of your morning routine.

There are other health benefits associated with this breathing exercise that goes by the name, **Pranayama**. Pranayama is the practice of breath regulation. It is a main component of yoga, an exercise meant for physical and mental wellness.

During this unique breathing exercise, you purposely inhale, exhale, and hold your breath in a specific sequence. Pranayama is an ancient practice of breath control, where you control the timing, duration and frequency of every breath and hold. The goal of pranayama is to connect your body and mind. It also enhances the supply of oxygen throughout your body while removing toxins. The entire exercise is meant to provide you with physiological healing benefits.

A research paper based on studies conducted on 50 adults, the subject being an attempt to know the effect of pranayama (Breathing exercise) over a period of 6 weeks, suggested the following results.

- It strengthens your lungs.
- It acts as a stress reliever.
- Improves concentration.
- Improves sleep quality.
- It boosts immunity
- It improves cardiovascular health.
- It improves digestion
- It makes the skin glow

For this exercise, you can allocate 5 minutes.

C. Affirmation (5 minutes)

The third-morning ritual during the victory hour is "affirmation". Many readers may wonder: What exactly is affirmation?. Affirmation is derived from the word "affirm, " meaning you believe something is true and strongly support it.

Moreover, you are giving that thing a big nod. If you maintain this mindset in your daily life, I can vouch that your dreams will come true and you will become the person you wish to be. Yes, you heard me right. You must believe you are the person the world wants to see become great and tell your mind as much.

As a reader, your dream might be to become a company's successful CEO or the best employee and reach the highest rank in your dream career. You can achieve this and more through affirmations. Mike Tyson used to affirm daily that he was the no. 1 champion in Boxing. Repeating these words everyday rewired his mind, and his brain started to believe it. Soon, he became the world champion in boxing. This kind of success through affirmation is applicable to anyone.

If you are a professional and want to be the best in your field, you can affirm daily that you are your organization's shining star and the best employee. In affirmation, you must continuously verbalize from your heart the positive thoughts you have regarding what you want to achieve. You have to say those thoughts aloud as if you have already succeeded. You must train your mind and brain to believe that you are on the path to achieving your wishes and that those thoughts are now your life's actual situation.

Research shows that MRI findings suggest specific neural pathways increase when people practice self-affirmation (Cascio et al.,1516). If you want to be super specific, you can say the ventromedial prefrontal cortex- involved in positive valuation and self-related information processing -becomes more active when we consider our values (Falk et al.,1515; Cascio et al.,1516).

Practice affirmation daily for 5 minutes as one of the morning victory hour rituals to become an extraordinary person.

D. Visualization (5 minutes)

The fourth-morning ritual in your victory hour is "visualization". Visualization is an ancient technique practised by many of the universe' successful people. The technique, also called the law of attraction, is suggested for your morning routine because it helps you turn your dream into reality. It helps your thoughts inspire and attract great dreams. I will tell you in detail how best to practice this technique.

Learning the technique will help you slowly appreciate opportunities the universe presents you. Consequently, you will be open to taking advantage of the emerging benefits. In short, you will become aware of available opportunities and immediately start taking advantage of them. You will appreciate for the realization of the miracle you have been waiting for, and things will start moving in your desired direction. This series of events has always worked and is still working for thousands of people.

In his book "Awaken the Giant Inside" Tony Robbins gives the example of Mike Tyson. Tyson wanted to become the best boxer in the world and be feted as the number one boxing champion. He followed the principle of visualization, where every day he would visualize himself as the best boxer in the world. He visualized getting victory after victory and bagging medals, time and again he would crush opponents and be declared champion. Ultimately, the world witnessed Mike Tyson becoming the world Boxing champion. His dream had turned into reality.

Many successful people have realized this power of attraction. They started by practising visualization in their daily work, and slowly they found things working to their advantage. Hence, day after day they found themselves on the path to success.

Visualization makes your familiar situation clearer, and once you can apply the technique just mentioned, you are bound to achieve the task you want. Suppose you have to give a presentation to your boss or client. You can visualize the entire process in your mind, where you foresee everyone in the conference room giving you a thumbs-up for your beautiful presentation. Practice this kind of visualization and you will be fulfilled even before you grab success. You will feel yourself conquering real situations. When you succeed in an actual event, this becomes your second victory, the first victory having been already won in your mind.

From today henceforth, set aside five minutes for your visualization process. This is one of the morning rituals you need to practice daily for 5 minutes, and you will see the magnificent difference in your life.

5. Meditation (5 minutes)

The fifth-morning ritual in your victory hour is "Meditation". The mind has the habit of wandering here and there, but meditation, the fifth morning ritual, can solve the challenge of the mind's wavering slides. You might have heard and read much about meditation, but for me, meditation means pure silence of the mind.

This quietness is essential to calming the mind because often the mind drifts so far away from positivity that it becomes challenging to focus on creativity. That is why the human mind is referred to as "Monkey Mind". Monkeys have the habit of jumping from one tree branch to another, and they are never at peace. They keep skipping from one activity to another in no logical manner. The human mind can be compared to that monkey behavior. It is never stable and keeps wandering.

You may recall your mind taking you back to your past days, probably bringing back thoughts of sadness. If such thoughts of past unpleasant events persist, you are likely to feel gloomy. The mind tends to fall back to the past and bring you events that have already occurred, and you get trapped in those thoughts. Whereas everyone falls victim to these flashbacks where events of the past come flooding your mind, there is a way you can control your mind. You may be wondering: Can we really mold our minds as we wish? Can we condition our minds to harbor only positive thoughts? Yes, we can - such control is possible.

Research has confirmed the beneficial aspects of meditation. In addition to having better focus and control over their emotions, many people who meditate regularly have reduced levels of stress and bolstered immune systems. In a study published in the journal "Neuroimage", researchers report that certain regions of the brain of long-term meditators were larger than those of people in a similar control group. Specifically, meditators showed significantly larger volumes of the hippocampus and areas within the orbitofrontal cortex, the thalamus, and the inferior temporal gyrus - all

regions known for regulating emotions.

During meditation, sit with your back straight, close your eyes and concentrate on your breath. Concentrate on your breath as you inhale and exhale as you keep your eyes closed. Initially you may have trouble focusing on your breath, and remaining seated even for one minute becomes very tiring. But don't worry. Initially everyone faces this challenge. Slowly by slowly you will get used to it.

When you begin meditating for the first time, you will experience different thoughts visiting your mind, and you may get carried away by those thoughts. This is quite natural, and your only solution for such wandering thoughts is to accept them and let them go. Imagine thoughts as clouds and let those clouds of thoughts flow away. Avoid getting attached to the thoughts. As the numerous thoughts come and go like clouds, focus on your breathing. Feel how your belly inflates and deflates with every breath you take in and out. Continue concentrating on your breathing for the entire 5 minutes and I assure you there is a lot to gain. You will experience a difference in your life, and the problem which was initially disturbing you will now have a solution. This will be the start of an enjoyable life for you.

When you are able to tame your thoughts, you attract happiness and wealth, and gradually you begin to reflect radiance on your face. You need to experience this. Whatever age you are, you can meditate by either sitting with your legs crossed as you keep your back straight. Alternatively, if you are not comfortable sitting cross-legged, you can sit on a chair with your back straight as you concentrate on your breath. Find a peaceful location in your house and do this exercise for 5 minutes daily.

6. Reading (10 minutes)

The sixth-morning ritual in your victory hour is "Reading". Reading is very important in life, and when I say reading, I mean reading motivational or self-help books in the morning for 10 minutes.

Reading books will change you and set the tone for your day, enriching your mind with positive thoughts. I have personally experienced the change reading occasions, and I can say for sure you will develop positive vibes if you make morning reading your thing. Something else is that you start to be optimistic about life.

Since you are trying to develop a habit, take into account it takes 21 days to change old habits and to form an entirely new habit. Start reading any motivational book for at least 10 minutes as a matter of habit, every day after you have completed your meditation process. Do not worry about the number of pages you will have read within those 10 minutes. Initially you may manage to read one or two pages during that time, but whatever you read, do it with total concentration and try to understand what the author wants you to understand.

I can say books are one-on-one communication where the author converses with you. You can feel the author's thought process. Books are written based on the author's many experiences, and he/she brings in many research ideas from different sources.

Try to immerse yourself in the books and slowly imbibe the excellent habits and thoughts discussed. I assure you it will be empowering to read self-help books in the morning. You can purchase any motivational book and start reading right away. Maintain consistency reading 10 minutes every day, and slowly you will experience the compound effect of completing the book in a few days. Whatever book you purchase, finish it to the end. You should buy another book only when you have completed the first one or feel satisfied with the concepts in the book you are reading.

Research shows that 85% of all readers concentrate only on the first ten to eleven pages and then abandon the book. This is an incorrect way to handle early morning reading. Personally, I read self-help books for 10 minutes every day after completing my meditation ritual, and so far, I have completed 40 motivational books. It is exciting to learn something new every day from the fresh thoughts the book ignites.

From my experience, I can assure you once you get into the 10-minute morning reading habit, you will start to develop an interest in self-help books, and soon reading will become your hobby. Adopting reading as a hobby should be a victory for you as it will significantly change you for the better. You will develop a positive outlook to life, and in any situation, you will have the clarity to recognize if something is right or wrong.

Reading books always calms your mind. Purchase a book marker and put it on the page you have reached every single day. This will guide you as to where to start reading from the next morning. For convenience, you can set the timer on your mobile phone for the alarm to go off after 10 minutes. Stop reading when the alarm goes off, and then, with a pencil or pen, mark the spot where you have reached reading; from where you will start reading the following morning. It helps you become disciplined and brings an inquisitiveness to read what is next for another beautiful morning. Enjoy reading and become learned.

7. Free Writing (5 minutes)

The seventh-morning ritual in your victory hour is "Free Writing", which has tremendous power to turn your mindset into one of positivity. You need a positive mindset to begin connecting with yourself. I have read many self-help books and listened to different podcasts pertaining to morning writing, but I could not figure out precisely what and when to write in the morning. So, I set out to personally try some morning writing, and I kept adjusting my sequence of rituals. Ultimately, I found that free writing is the most suitable form of writing for morning, and it fits well at the end of my other morning victory rituals. This means free writing as part of the daily morning ritual is most beneficial after you have completed sweating exercise, breathing exercise , affirmation, visualization, meditation, and reading.

Why the term "free" writing? I call this form of writing "free writing" because you write whatever comes to your mind. It may be your emotions or an event that occurred in your life. The reality is that 5 minutes of daily free writing will change you. When it comes to writing, I have had personal experience writing in a dairy. A diary has dates and this makes you accountable in ensuring you write on a daily basis.

Just write whatever comes to your mind without worrying about grammatical or spelling mistakes. You cannot have everything right the same day. Besides, this free writing is neither a competition nor an article you are writing for publication. You are simply writing down your thoughts as they run through your mind and the most important aspect is that you are letting those thoughts flow in writing. Just keep on writing for 5 continuous minutes, and I can guarantee you will soon find yourself communicating with the one person you have never spoken to: you!

Research shows that writing declutters the mind and leaves it free and relaxed. That is why you should make up your mind to write every day for five minutes about any idea that comes to mind. Still, you can use these examples to guide you on what to write about.

- Write down what you have achieved by waking up early in the morning

- Write down what you have achieved by adhering to the morning victory hour rituals.

- Write about the learning from the book you are reading that day for your morning ritual

You can also write about something good happening in your life, your dreams, and your future plans.

Writing is communicating with oneself, and by expressing your thoughts on paper ends up releasing thoughts that would otherwise keep revolving in your mind. Personally, I write three to four pages in 5 minutes. So far, I have more than 50 notebooks I have written as a part of my daily free-writing habit.

8. Plan Your Day (10 minutes)

The eighth-morning ritual in your victory hour is "Planning your day". The path to becoming an extraordinary person starts with strategic planning. If your planning is good, you will be the king in your area of operation. But to attain this planning mindset, your brain has to work at its utmost capacity, which is only possible if you religiously follow the morning rituals contained in this book.

We require planning to make our day bright in whatever phase of life we are in. Whether you're a Sales professional, Marketing professional , HR ,CEO of a company etc., you need to plan well as you start your day, so that everything you encounter gets aligned with your expectations for the day. In short, proper and timely planning gives you immense power as you start your day, because you are conscious about what is essential and what you want to execute.

Planning does not mean you manage to plan all the work you will ever do on the same day. It only means you are prepared to tackle the most important tasks first. In planning, you prioritize the most important assignment for the day.

In the book by Brian Tracy, "Eat That Frog", the author talks about eating first the ugliest frog; eating the ugliest of them early in the morning. Once you have accomplished this, any other frog lined up for you will be a walk in the park. In other words, you are bound to find your day's tasks easy to deal with once you begin with the toughest. Here, the ugliest frog means the work that is very important or challenging.

In Chapter 6, I have covered planning and prioritization in detail, where you will learn various techniques that can ease your planning. During the morning victory hour, I strongly recommend allocating 10 minutes to meticulous planning of your day. Close your eyes and think of the task at hand and then jot down the tasks you consider to be of topmost importance for that day. Stick to your plan. Practising this habit daily will lead you to become productive in your work, and you will own the day.

Key takeaways

Based on extensive research and experiments I have personally done, I recommend the 8 morning rituals, which get you fully charged for the day within 60 minutes. This 60-minute period immediately after you wake up is your "ME-time", and I call it "VICTORY HOUR". Follow the morning rituals in the order given below:

Sl. no	Morning Ritual	Time Duration
01.	Exercise	15 minutes
02.	Breathing Exercise	5 minutes
03.	Affirmation	5 minutes
04.	Visualization	5 minutes
05.	Meditation	5 minutes
06.	Reading	10 minutes
07.	Free Writing	5 minutes
08.	Planning your day	10 minutes
Total time duration		**60 minutes**

Chapter Five

Productivity Hacks –How to Maximize your time and Efficiency.

> **"Productivity is never an accident. It is always the result of a commitment to excellence, intelligent planning and focused effort".**
>
> **Paul J. Meyer**

In today's hectic world, it is crucial to prioritize your time and work in order to efficiently get the utmost output. Time is of the essence and everyone has 24 hours in a day to perform. When we talk about office hours, we refer to 8 hrs to 9 hrs we spend in the office. This is when you need to invest yourself most in your assignment if you are to accomplish the task well. If you utilize your time as explained further in the chapter, you will slowly increase your efficiency and start going up the corporate ladder. But as you know, Rome was not built in a day, and this applies to your journey to developing efficient working habits.

In your organization, top management measures your performance on two Key Responsibility Areas (KRAs): your efficiency in meeting set targets and your interpersonal skills as you relate with your subordinates, colleagues, and boss. You will be judged and appraised on these parameters, and whoever meets the criteria set by top management receives a job promotion and rises up the corporate ladder. Still, it is vital to note that you may do what is required as you aspire to climb up the corporate ladder yet fail in the annual promotion process. You may not be granted any higher responsibility, designation, higher salary increment, or any additional perks. Why would this happen to you while a few of your colleagues have gotten promotions and are steadily climbing up the corporate ladder? It must be that the way you perform your job varies from the way they perform theirs. Research shows that all human beings have the same intelligence, some developing theirs over time. Still, others do not put the effort to develop theirs. It is the same way athletes have fit bodies while many of us do not, though we may be healthy. Why is it the case? The reason is that although you and the athlete both have the same physical features, the athlete has invested time to develop or fine-tune his body and you have not. You may not have maintained the discipline of eating the right food and exercising in the morning. Similarly, you need to train your mind to be disciplined and to be more productive at work. But as I told you in my previous chapter, you can change yourself by merely taking a decision.

You can also become as physically fit as an athlete or efficient in the office if you consciously decide to change yourself TODAY. You can be the blue-eyed boy of your organization or department if you follow the techniques I will be discussing in this chapter.

The technique I will talk about is research-based, and it has influenced many winners within organizations. The first and the foremost is not to get distracted while you work. You are not the only one in the workforce who gets distracted while you work. More than 90% of the population get distracted and are unable to concentrate on their jobs. There may be many reasons for this which may cause the distractions most people experience without realizing it, where they are unable to concentrate on their work. Here is a list of distractions that affect your office work:

1. Urge to frequently check your emails.
2. Urge to check messages on your mobile phone.
3. Urge to jump to social media platforms in between your work
4. Urge to check some data of previous meetings, which may not have relevance then.

According to research, these urges result from secretion of the hormone, "Dopamine", which causes you a pleasant feeling of anticipation. As your mind experiences this pleasure that gives you a sense of fulfilment, you end up being distracted with tasks such as checking your emails, social media accounts and so on.

To ensure you are not distracted, you must set a specific time for any activity you consider vital, and which you are determined to complete. Examples of important tasks that need to have their own slots in your schedule include review plans, important presentations, submission of projects with deadlines, and such. You need to concentrate on completing the assignment, yet often you find yourself getting distracted after you have started your work. These distractions may occur because of the mentioned urges to check mobile messages or incoming email notifications. Be aware that once you succumb to the first distraction you are likely to be dragged further to attend to other distracting tasks such as reading news or replying to emails. Eventually when you resume your scheduled work, you realize you have lost 20-25 minutes of your time.

You may be doing an assignment that requires total concentration, but the same cycle of distraction continues. Your colleague or support staff may enter your cabin, something you may not manage to deter, and at the end you will have lost your valuable productive time. This is a situation where you have failed to complete your essential assignment in time because of a distraction from someone else.

You are not the only one facing such distractions in your work. 90% of working people do, and they take responsibility for not completing their project in time. In their minds they admit they have failed and the following day they are more determined to complete the work.

The truth is that obstacles in workplace are uncertain, but there is a way to end your assignment in time; and completing a set assignment gives you satisfaction. By completing your assignment as planned, you would be more productive at work. The best strategy I suggest is to follow what is termed the "POMODORO" technique.

In this technique, you need to set 20 minutes of your time for the assignment you want to accomplish. To avoid interruptions, set the alarm to go off after 20 minutes. You can also download the "POMODORO" app from the app store and fix the time in the app. After 20 minutes, you can take a break of 5 minutes and then continue the next round of 20 minutes of assignment without disturbance.

During your 20-minute sessions, avoid distractions and instead concentrate deeply on your work. Once you can accomplish this, you are bound to feel the difference in your productivity. You will now finish faster many of the assignments that used to take you time to finish. You can apply this technique for any task you want to complete in scheduled time. Further, during the 5 minutes' break, you can relax, take tea/coffee, or take a walk around.

You can take a deep breath to relax your mind. After completing two rounds of 20 minutes of deep work without interruptions, you can take a longer break of 10-15 minutes. Thereafter you can now check your emails, or important phone messages. You can use this POMODORO technique effectively during office hours.

Multitasking is disastrous:

If you want to yield high productivity, you must handle one task at a time, something you cannot accomplish when making a presentation, attending to emails, and checking messages. In short, you cannot multitask if you want quality work output. According to Author Cal Newport, switching from one task to another as you multi-task reduces concentration and wastes time due to **ATTENTION RESIDUE.**

The term ATTENTION RESIDUE was first used by Sophie Leroy, associate professor at the University of Washington in her 2009 paper. She described the term as the thoughts that carry over from one unfinished task onto the next. Attention residue is also called mental residue. Every time you reply to an email and switch back to your presentation, a part of the email thoughts still remains in your head. As a result, your level of concentration is interfered with, and it can take a whole minute to resume working on the presentation with the required focus. Newport calls this type of work **"Shallow Work"** as you work with a distracted mind.

Multitasking is terrible for your brain because the brain is wired to handle one thing at a time. Can you imagine a doctor multitasking by checking emails or phone messages as he operates on you? Of course, this behavior would be hazardous. He must, of necessity, pay undivided attention to the operation he is performing.

Similarly, it would be disastrous for a pilot to multitask while flying an airplane. This is true of all professionals. They cannot carry out their work assignments while multi-tasking and expect the results to be great. This calls for deep work. Deep work is about being completely immersed in the task at hand. While at Deep Work, you focus on one task at a time the way an eagle concentrates on its prey. Long stretches of focused work can do wonders when it comes to result.

We all need to pay undivided attention to the task at hand if we are to deliver impressive projects results in a timely manner, and not carry home residual burden of unfinished work. For everyone, home should be spared for family, where our families receive 100% attention. While at home, we need to be present with our loved ones both mentally and physically.

Key takeaways

- Here is a list of common office distractions:
  - ✓ Urge to check emails frequently.
  - ✓ Urge to check messages on your mobile phone.
  - ✓ Urge to check social media platforms in between your work.
  - ✓ Urge to check some information from previous meetings, which may not be relevant then.
- These urges result from secretion of the hormone, "Dopamine", which generates a pleasant feeling that causes you anticipation.

- Follow the **"POMODORO"** technique, where you only need to set 20 uninterrupted minutes of your time for the assignment at hand.

- Working on multiple tasks by switching between tasks reduces concentration and wastes time due to **ATTENTION RESIDUE.** Attention residue comprises thoughts that carry over from one unfinished task into the next task.

- Every time you reply to an email and switch back to your presentation, some thoughts of the email are still in your head. As a result, your concentration is affected and it can take you a full minute to regain your presentation focus. This lack of concentration has a compound effect on overall productivity, which is essentially **SHALLOW WORK.**

Chapter Six

Planning and Prioritization: Organizing Your Tasks and Goals

> **"An hour of planning can save you 10 hours of doing."**
>
> **Dale Carnegie**

The path to becoming an extraordinary person starts with strategic planning. If your planning is good, you become the master in your area of operation. But to attain this planning mindset, your brain has to work at its full capacity. This is only possible when you religiously follow the morning rituals taught in Chapter 4 of this book.

We need to plan for our day if we are to make it bright in whatever phase of life that we find ourselves in. Proper planning at the start of the day gets everything aligned with your expectations. You will feel intensely driven because you will be prepared to tackle what is essential and to execute it.

Planning does not mean you manage to plan all the work you will ever do on the same day. It only means you are prepared to tackle the most important tasks first. You need to do the most important task first.

Again I reiterate the concepts talked about in the book by Brian Tracy, "Eat That Frog" where the author talks about eating first the ugliest frog, eating the ugliest of them early in the morning. Once you have accomplished this, any other frog lined up for you will be easy to tackle. In other words, you are bound to find later tasks easy to handle once you start off with the toughest. Here, the ugliest frog means the work that is very important or challenging.

I remember a small story which is an eye-opener for planning purposes, and the story goes like this:

There was once a businessman who sought advice to run a business and earn much profit. A town consultant offered to help him. However, the consultant demanded the businessman first give him 10 million dollars, and after that he would hand over a sealed envelope with a written solution enclosed inside. The consultant also promised the businessman that he would return 10 million dollars if the businessman did not like the answer. The businessman accepted the consultant's offer and the conditions. The businessman paid the consultant 10 million dollars as per the agreement and immediately received the sealed envelope.

The businessman opened the sealed envelope and found white piece of paper inside with only one sentence written on it: "Write five important tasks you want to do today and stick to it". On reading this line, the businessman smiled, agreed to part with the money, and thanked the consultant for opening his eyes. He concurred with him that the solution was worth more than 10 million dollars.

This solution seems very simple and obvious as a success strategy, but many people who know it do not follow it. This reality makes the difference between a successful and not-so-successful individual. If you stick to your day's planning whatever happens in the day, then nobody can beat you in the race for success. We often plan and write down in our diary important tasks to be accomplished, but we still have residual tasks carried over to the following day. Failure to complete such tasks is not caused by absence from the office, but a change in priorities. We get carried away with emerging issues, and we end up tackling tasks as they appear before us.

I strongly recommend you plan your day during 10 minutes of your morning victory hour. Close your eyes, think of the task at hand, and jot down the topmost important assignments on a piece of paper. Practising this habit on a daily basis will make you productive in your work, and you will have control of your day.

When I started my career, I found it challenging to prioritize my work as everything felt like a priority. It was always a challenge for me to identify which task I should accomplish first and which one should follow. I did not focus much on results as all the tasks, in my view, were of equal importance. After a few years of working haphazardly, I discovered, to my relief, the **"Eisenhower Matrix".**, To date, I am strictly following this principle.

The Eisenhower Matrix is a productivity, prioritization, and time-management framework designed to help you prioritize tasks or agenda items by categorizing them according to their urgency and importance.

I have tried out this principle with my own work, and it has been giving me great results. I am now stress free and have ample time to concentrate on other important work. I will tell you exactly what Matrix is, and how you can replicate the same success in your career to become more successful in your area of operation.

Eisenhower Matrix

	URGENT	NOT URGENT
IMPORTANT	**DO** Deadlines True crisis	**PLAN** Strategic Thinking
NOT IMPORTANT	**DELEGATE** Some emails Some Phone calls Some interruptions	**STOP** Internet Surfing

Analysis of Matrix

First Quadrant (upper left)	Urgent and Important
Second Quadrant (upper right)	Important but not Urgent
Third Quadrant (lower left)	Not Important, but Urgent
Fourth Quadrant (lower right)	Neither Important nor Urgent

In the first quadrant, you must do only the urgent and important work. Urgent and important means the work cannot be ignored and needs immediate attention. Generally, such tasks include the assignments from the organization's top management or your immediate boss, and it requires close attention and prompt action.

The general tendency is for people to procrastinate such tasks and to attend to them at leisure or as time permits. This tendency is suicidal and the thinking behind it ought to be checked. Similar tasks include presentations with deadlines. These should be attended to as a matter of top priority.

The Second quadrant includes important but not urgent activities. Such tasks may consist of strategic or general planning of your work. Planning is essential as it is the pillar for the organization's success, but it is not urgent enough to be tackled before all other jobs. Planning requires thinking, and relatively good planning requires SLOW THINKING. At work, planning may be a three-year or five-year road map of the KRA you are responsible for. At a personal level, planning areas may include vacations, medical checkups, and such functions that occur annually. The idea is to categorize your work according to the urgency of every task.

The third quadrant includes those urgent but unimportant activities. These activities are no doubt urgent, but they are not that important as to take precedence over all other work. The work within the 3rd quadrant may include checking emails and making phone calls and such other tasks often considered interruptions.

It is upon you to make a good judgement on when the task involved can be managed. Alternatively, you can delegate such work to your co-workers. For example, you can ask them to respond to your work-related emails or receive phone calls from clients.

The fourth quadrant includes those activities that are neither urgent nor important; those tasks that you can ignore without any risk. These include the types of things you undertake to distract yourself from serious work or thoughts. Often people engage in these tasks because they lead to significant release of dopamine, which makes the activity pleasurable. The activities may include surfing the internet, checking personal emails, or any activity unrelated to your work. I recommend you avoid activities in this category during working hours.

On the overall, it is advisable to figure out the importance of every piece of work and to deal with it accordingly. You are best placed to judge the importance of every task before you and doing it right can take you to the fast lane.

I have read many books on top performers and listened to various podcasts on how to increase the productivity of the employee workforce. Further, I have conducted different analyses regarding the best possible outcome from multiple theories discussed. I have personally tried out the same principles and theories in my career for the last 24 years, and found a few of the postulates to be accurate. Hence, I have continued following them with exemplary results. I am satisfied with my work-life balance, and I recommend you and other professionals to follow these principles in true spirit in all areas of operation.

The 80/20 Principle is one such principle that I continue to follow, and I strongly advocate that you make the effort to understand it well, and then to adopt it for a successful career.

In 1920, Vilfredo Pareto discovered the 80/20 principle, also known as the Pareto's principle. Pareto found out that just like there is a universal truth in the Law of Gravity, there is also a truth behind the pattern of 80/20. He observed that 80% of the world's wealth is in the hands of 20% of the people, who are all successful in life. Later, he realized that this pattern is true for any activity, as 80% of the crimes happen because of 20% of the criminals, 80% of an organization's profits is contributed by 20% of the products, and 80% of an organization's productivity is contributed by 20% of the staff. There are numerous similar examples where the 80/20 principle is applicable.

Sometimes this principle can vary as 90/10 or 70/30. Most executives put much effort into their work but still do not get recognition for it. They are late sitters and believe late sitting will bring in the result. But it never happens. Why? Because they do not work smart.

Management recognizes those workers who do their work efficiently within the Turnaround time (TAT). There may be several tasks before you, or there may be a huge target to achieve, but even after you are done you will realize that only 20% of the work has produced immediate results; and this is the proportion that will earn you recognition.

Recognition at the workplace boosts your self-esteem and gives you a feel-good factor. Consequently, you feel motivated from within and remain so for quite a while. Aim to finish that crucial 20% of the work and thereafter you can embark on the remaining 80%; and only if you think it is worthwhile. You may wish to adopt the strategy of delegating tasks as already discussed.

Please keep in mind to the importance of working smart ,if you want to grow in the organization. In the end, what matters is the quality output you contribute to the organization. If you have a sales target, you can concentrate on those territories or pockets where your product sells well, and a little push from your side can reach 80% of the target. You need to determine which 20% of the products will bring you closer to your target.

Another postulate with which I am fascinated is Parkinson's Law, which states that work will expand till it fills the time allotted for its completion. Our behavior is built around Parkinson's law which is close to each of us. Still, since events are part and parcel of our daily life, we take our behavior for granted and keep compromising on available possibilities. Ultimately, because of our tendency to procrastinate, we keep on delaying to act. But I discovered a science behind our behavior when I read Parkinson's law. I want my readers to fully understand the essence of this law, so that after reading this chapter you will feel you have gained important knowledge which was, nevertheless, within you all along.

Cyril Northcote Parkinson first coined the term "Parkinson's Law" in a humorous essay he wrote for "The Economist" in 1955. In the essay he shares the story of a woman whose only task in a day was to send a postcard, a task that would take an active person approximately three minutes. However, the woman would spend an hour locating the card, another half hour looking for her eye glasses, 90 minutes writing the card, 20 minutes trying to decide whether or not to take an umbrella along on her walk to the mailbox …., and on and on until her day was completely filled with activities revolving around the single task. This analogy is applicable to any assignment or project we undertake without a vision.

Generally, office assignments are set to be completed in a week or a month according to the intensity or demands of the work involved. Even if the work is of small magnitude, it is possible to expand it over trivial issues, until the set week or month comes to an end. In short, we can make the project occupy the official time even when it is possible to accomplish it within a shorter period. Sometimes, work that is extended unnecessarily longer end up not seeing the light of day.

Taking clues from **Parkinson's Law,** we can fix a date for completing the job and make it sacrosanct.

We should achieve this by assessing the work and planning well to determine the man-days and effort required to finish the work. Equipped with this information, we can then fix a reasonable deadline by which to complete the work. The estimated date should be practical. It should be set after taking into consideration applicable factors and leaving a 30% margin of error.

For example, if we estimate that a specific project or assignment will be completed in 7 days, we can keep a buffer of 30%, hence setting job completion time at ten days. This added time allowance is important because we are not sure what obstacles may arise. After all, many things are beyond our control. Sometimes work depends on other stakeholders within the organization, which makes it difficult to control what happens. At the end of the day, you should set a precise date for job completion. It is great to complete the work well within the deadline to your satisfaction and the delight top management, but in no way should you try to extend the deadline once you have set it.

In my initial career, I faced many obstacles in achieving my set target. I have subsequently found that those obstacles were the barriers in my mindset that kept delaying the process. As I sought to excel in my career, I discovered **Yerkes-Dodson Law** which states that there is an optimal level of arousal responsible for improving task performance. There is a relationship between arousal and behavioral task performance, such that for optimal performance there must be optimal level of arousal. Over or under-arousal reduces task performance. So, that fast-approaching end date gives us a much-needed kick to start the work.

Suppose we combine Parkinson's Law and Yerkes-Dodson Law. We find that the fast-approaching date of assignment completion sets off the adrenaline rush, and your arousal level rises. Your performance is at its peak when your mind is aroused to the optimal level. Any less than the optimum level of arousal will lead to you performing below par, and any arousal that rises beyond the optimum again interferes with your performance. This means you must keep your mind charged to the extent it enables you perform your work with a balanced mindset where you are neither too excited nor too unexcited.

Therefore, setting a deadline is mandatory for completion of any work, and you should put utmost effort into completing the work within the target date. Once you inculcate the habit of setting timelines and keeping to them, you will become a top performer and no-one can stop you from reaching the pinnacle of your career.

Key takeaways

- Adopt the Eisenhower Matrix in your work. The matrix is a productivity, prioritization, and time-management framework designed to help you prioritize tasks or agenda items by categorizing them according to their urgency and importance.

- Classify your work into **Urgent and Not Urgent & Important and Not Important**.

- Determine which 20% of the work will produce 80% of the result.

- Believe in **Parkinson's Law** which states that work will expand to fill the time allotted for its completion.

- Understand the human mindset through **Yerkes-Dodson ,** which states there is an optimal level of arousal that improves task performance. There is a relationship between arousal and behavioral task performance, such that there is an optimal level of arousal for optimal performance. Over or under-arousal reduces task performance. Fast-approaching end date gives us a much-needed kick to start the work.

Chapter Seven

Conclusion

> **"Whenever you are asked if you can do a job, tell them, "Certainly I Can!" Then get busy and find out how to do it".**
>
> **Theodore Roosevelt**

Key takeaways

Chapter 1: Introduction

- "If anyone can do it successfully, you, too, can do it".

- Success always leaves clues, and you need to follow those clues for you to succeed.

- Faith, burning desire, and consistency, abbreviated as FBC, will move the mountains.

- You have a hidden potential within you that was asleep till now. This hidden potential is your **"SLEEPING GIANT"**. You can awaken it.

Key Takeaways

Chapter 2: The Power of the Morning Hour

Waking up early can positively impact your physical and mental health as well as your productivity and overall quality of life. Research has shown that waking up early in the morning can have a variety of benefits:

- Increased productivity: Waking up early gives you more time to plan your day and get things done. Research has shown that people who wake up early are more productive than those who wake up later in the day.

- Better mental health: Studies have shown that waking up early is associated with better mental health, including lower stress levels, anxiety, and depression.

- Improved sleep quality: Going to bed and waking up at the same time each day helps regulate your body's internal clock and improve the quality of your sleep.

- Better physical health: People who wake up early tend to be more active and engage in more physical activity, resulting in a range of health benefits. Such benefits include lowering the risk of obesity, diabetes, and heart disease.

- More time for self-care: Waking up early gives you more time to take care of yourself, whether exercising, meditating, or enjoying a quiet cup of coffee before the day starts.

Key Takeaways

Chapter 3- Setting the Stage for Success: Preparing for Your Morning Routine

- Set your alarm time initially as it suits you, either for 5.30 a.m. or 6 a.m. and wake up every day at the same time.

- Wake up at the ring of the first alarm and do not succumb to the slightest temptation to press the snooze button.

- Keep the alarm clock a distance from your bed so that you will need to walk up that distance to stop the alarm.

- Do not look back at your bed once you have risen. Instead, leave the bedroom immediately and proceed to the kitchen to take a glass of water.

- Drinking a glass of water after you wake up immediately hydrates your body, which is important as your body loses water after a span of 6-7 hours of sleep.

Key Takeaways

Chapter 4: Mindset Matters: How to start your day with a Positive Attitude

Based on my extensive research and personal experiments, I recommend the 8 morning rituals, which take 60 minutes to make you fully charged for the day. The 60 minutes immediately after you wake up is your "ME" time; the period I call "VICTORY HOUR". Follow the morning rituals in the order given below:

Sl. no	Morning Ritual	Time Duration
01.	Exercise	15 minutes
02.	Breathing Exercise	5 minutes
03.	Affirmation	5 minutes
04.	Visualization	5 minutes
05.	Meditation	5 minutes
06.	Reading	10 minutes

07.	Free Writing	5 minutes
08.	Planning your day	10 minutes
Total time duration		**60 minutes**

Key Takeaways

Chapter 5   Productivity Hacks – How to Maximize your time and Efficiency

- Here is a list of distractions you often encounter in the office:

  ✓ Urge to check emails frequently.

  ✓ Urge to check messages on your mobile phone

  ✓ Urge to check social media platforms in between your work

- ✓ Urge to check some data from previous meetings, which may not be currently relevant.

- These urges result from the hormone "dopamine" secretion, which generates a pleasant feeling in the hope of raising anticipation.

- Follow the "**POMODORO**" technique where you set aside 20 minutes of your time for the assignment you want to do without interruptions.

- Working on multiple tasks by switching between tasks reduces concentration and wastes time due to **ATTENTION RESIDUE.** Attention Residue are thoughts that carry over from one unfinished task to the next.

- Every time you reply to an email and switch back to your presentation, partial thoughts of that email remain in your head. As a result, your concentration is affected, and it can take you extra minutes to regain enough focus to enable you complete the presentation. This mode of working has a compound effect on overall productivity. It results in **SHALLOW WORK.**

- Deep work is about being completely immersed in the task at hand. While at Deep Work, you focus on one task at a time the way an eagle concentrates on its prey.

Key Takeaways

**Chapter 6: Planning and Prioritization:
How to Organize Your Tasks and Goals**

- Adopt Eisenhower Matrix in your work. The matrix comprises productivity, prioritization, and a time-management framework, designed to help you prioritize tasks or agenda items by categorizing them according to their urgency and importance.

- Classify your work into **Urgent and Not Urgent & Important and Not Important**.

- You need to determine the 20% of your work likely to contribute 80% of the result.

- Believe in **Parkinson's Law** which states that work will expand to fill the time allotted for its completion.

- Understand the human mindset through **Yerkes-Dodson Law** which says there is an optimal level of arousal that improves task performance. There is a direct relationship between arousal and behavioural task performance, such that the optimal level of arousal corresponds to optimal performance. Over or under-arousal reduces task performance. Fast-approaching end date gives us a much-needed kick to start the work.

Feedback

I would love to know your thoughts on this book. I will be all ears waiting to hear your feedback, because I am aware there is always room for improvement. I will listen to negative comments with an open mind and try to address your concerns. Please drop me an email at gyansnarayan22@gmail.com.

I look forward to hearing from you. Also, if you liked this book, do not forget to leave a review.

Meanwhile, it is my belief this book will help the world become a more productive place.

GRAB YOUR VICTORY HOUR

LEARN TECHNIQUES OF 60 MINUTES MORNING RITUALS THAT WILL TRANSFORM YOU TO AN EXTRAORDINARY PERSON

GYAN S NARAYAN

Acknowledgement

I thank my parents, who have inculcated in me a good habit of reading books, making it possible to compile this book. I am highly indebted to my wife, Sanchita, who has always encouraged me to write down for the sake of other people, the lessons I practice by listening to various podcasts and reading self-help books. This book would not have been possible without her support and the sacrifices she has made, including allowing me to write the book in solitude on weekends.

I would also like to acknowledge the sacrifice my little daughter, Ishanvi, has made, as she has refrained from demanding to play with me whenever she has found me writing the manuscript. Sanchita and Ishanvi – I love you both!

Copyright

.

www.ingramcontent.com/pod-product-compliance
Lightning Source LLC
Chambersburg PA
CBHW070357220526
45467CB00001B/419